Steps to Holiness

Carla Burton

Dedication

To my parents, Carl & JoAnn Varnell, who taught me the steps and then showed me how to walk in them every day. Your example is my path.

Carla Burton

Contents

Preface

Being raised in the church all my life, I have always obediently and to the best of my ability followed holiness standards. However, when my husband and I took our present church in Nashville, Tennessee, I began to realize that I was going to be teaching others how they should live. Feeling the great responsibility of teaching God's Word correctly, I began a personal study into the subject of holiness. During this time, the Lord gave me great revelation concerning the process of holiness. I began to understand that what I believed was all correct, however, I had obeyed it all in the wrong order.

I have written this booklet so that anyone, a new convert or a long-time Christian, can study and understand the order and importance of every aspect of holiness. My greatest desire is that through this booklet, you will be able to walk in holiness with great joy and understanding.

There are several other booklets in this series; however, we must start with the order that God intended concerning holiness. I trust that after reading this booklet you will not only understand, but you will have a greater respect for why you live as you do.

Chapter 1

An *Open Heart*

They say that there are three things that you never discuss unless you want to debate and they are: money, politics and religion. These are three areas that people have very definite opinions and are usually extremely verbal in expressing them. But if we take that same principle and define it within the Christian community, there is one topic that most Christian have very "strong opinions" regarding – holiness. I have heard people, who never spoke up regarding any other Biblical subject have a vocal and defined opinion regarding this topic.

I believe that having a strong opinion is a great thing on any subject, as long as you have the right Biblical basis and understanding to back up your opinion. We have gotten ourselves in trouble throughout the history of man, by walking according to our own understanding rather than according to the Word of God.

There is a difference between being a hearer and a doer of the Word. But what is the difference? I believe that being a doer comes down to not just hearing and believing in the Word but also receiving an illumination of the principle and purpose of the commandment and then obedience follows.

For God to get His Word from creation to the Bible that we hold in our hands today, He had to create a process. There were three steps He used to accomplish this task.

- ➢ Revelation – from God to man *(man hears what God wants written)*
- ➢ Inspiration – from man to paper *(man becomes the scribe for God and writes what He wants told)*
- ➢ Illumination – from paper to heart *(man receives and obeys that which is written)*

It is not enough that we just have a revelation that God wants to tell us something or even an inspiration to read what has already been written, but we must have a personal, intense illumination from the Word for us to become obedient.

The apostle Paul was a perfect example of this in Acts chapter nine. Paul was raised a strict Pharisee and when he was approximately fourteen sent to Jerusalem to become a rabbi. He sat and learned at the feet of Gamaliel, one of the most prominent teachers of that day. He grew up strong in his belief that the Holy Scriptures were given by revelation of God and he never questioned the men who had written these Scriptures through inspiration. But Paul still did not have an illumination of Jesus Christ. However, following his experience on the road to Damascus, Paul becomes a man of understanding and obedience. This new illuminated Paul was so adamant about this that he wrote the following in Galatians 1:8-9, *"But though we, or an angel from heaven, preach any other gospel unto you than that which we have preached unto you, let him be accursed. As we said before, so say I now again, If any man preach any other gospel unto you than that you have received, let him be accursed."* These are truly the words of a man who has received a divine illumination regarding the Scriptures.

The purpose of this booklet is not to give you a personal opinion regarding holiness but rather to give you a guide *from the Bible* to help you find illumination. All I ask is that as you walk through this process of holiness that you sincerely, earnestly and with an open heart and mind, seek understanding regarding this topic. Allow the written Word to become illuminated in your heart through the process of study and then your actions will follow.

Chapter 2

Submission *to Authority*

The Bible has one theme throughout its entirety and that is submitting our will to the will of God and the authority that He places in our lives. I will never be able in this chapter to give you a complete, Biblical understanding of authority and the importance of your submission to that authority, but you do need to understand the purpose of submission in regards to holiness.

First of all I would like to make myself clear regarding this booklet and the authority of your Pastor. My desire, in this booklet, is to give you knowledge and understanding but not to give you a tool to use against your Shepherd. God has placed the man of God in our lives to lead, guide and instruct us in the ways of righteousness more perfectly. There may be standards discussed here, that your Pastor has required something more or different from you and your church. It is very important that you remember that God placed you in that flock and under that Shepherd to guide your life and the *greatest holiness standard you can follow is submission to the authority* in your life! Now, let me be very clear here, if your pastoral authority is asking you to do things that cannot be backed up by Scripture, or the importance to the overall good of your local assembly cannot be explained, then you need to seek the counsel of godly men and through prayer and fasting make a decision regarding this. However, if your Pastor is teaching you from the Word of God and the problem is that you don't agree but cannot back it up Biblical, then you need to check *your* spirit. That is a spirit of rebellion and you need to be sure that you are submitted to the godly authority in your life.

I remember when I was growing up, one Sunday my Pastor, T. L. Craft from Jackson, Mississippi got up and his sermon that day was, "Thou Shalt Not Play Rook!" Of course, the entire church sat up and took notice because this was a favorite game of the young married couples and the singles. But our Pastor went on to explain by telling us that this was not a heaven or hell standard but that this was a request by him that we would abstain from this on a temporary basis. He further elaborated by saying that the reason he did this was because our young married and singles were staying up on Saturday nights until the wee hours of the morning playing marathon Rook games and then sleeping in and missing church and their ministry duties on Sunday morning. He used scriptures about faithfulness, the Bible's command to not miss the opportunity to assemble in a church environment, the Old Testament scriptures about placing other "idols" before your relationship with God.

Now you may think that is ridiculous or he should not have done that. I disagree with you. God had placed that man in charge of the spiritual wellbeing of those saints. He was going to have to give an account for their souls and his desire was to be able to do it with joy and not sorrow (Hebrews 13:17). The true test of this message was that God began, at that moment, testing the submission of the people to the godly authority placed in their lives.   Submission to godly, Biblical-based authority is as important, sometimes more important, than the standard.   What I mean is that sometimes God sets the "issue and/or standard" aside to deal with the concept of submission to authority in your life.

I want to be sure that you understand how important the issue of spiritual authority is to me because I never want this book to be used as a tool against your Pastor.   No matter my personal opinion, God has placed that man of God in your life and you should respect, love and follow his instructions.   This book is simply a tool to help you find the Biblical basis for why we believe what we believe and to help you understand the principle behind the issue. This is not a tool to help you subvert spiritual authority in your life.

Chapter 3

Order *by God*

God plans *everything.* In I Corinthians 14:40 the Apostle Paul insists, *"Let all things be done decently and in order."* Even before the world was created, God knew exactly how He would order the planets, how He would have to redeem the world back unto Himself, and how He would have to dwell in man to help him maintain order in his walk with God upon this earth.

There is power in God's order. Read Ecclesiastes 3:1-8. The scripture explains how God has ordered the seasons of life. He has given everything a time, place, and way. We must never underestimate the power of God's order. We must not rush the times of weeping, mourning, breaking down, and war because without those things in their order we could not have laughing, dancing, building up, and love.

Here are some examples of things God has set in order: the seasons (Ecclesiastes 3:1); the Solar System and ecological systems (Genesis 1:15-17; Psalms 8:3); and the chain of authority of God-Man-Woman (Genesis 1-3 and I Corinthians 11:2-3).

God has also ordered steps to inward and outward holiness. The steps, in the following order, are attitude, principles, and then standards.

Carla Burton

Chapter 4

Defining *the Steps*

Attitude

An attitude is "a mental position or feeling with regard to a fact or state; the position of something in relation to something else." (*Webster's Dictionary*, Landoll, 1997) An attitude involves an understanding that holiness is a part of God and a part of Himself that He wants to give to us. Only when we have that understanding can we fulfill the second half of the definition of attitude—relating it to something else. When our minds take on an attitude of holiness, then we can relate that attitude to our daily lives and actually produce a holy lifestyle.

Principles

A principle is "a fundamental law, doctrine, or assumption; a rule or code of conduct and a devotion to that conduct; a primary source; an active source." (*Webster's Dictionary*, Landoll, 1997) A principle involves our knowledge and reason for following a code of conduct. It is the underlying law or doctrine that we understand and then obey according to our understanding. Once we understand the doctrine or law, then we can apply the second part of the definition of principle to our lives. When we have the knowledge, then it becomes the primary source that activates our lifestyle.

Standards

A standard is "something set up as a rule for measuring or as a model to be followed." (*Webster's Dictionary*, Landoll, 1997) A standard involves a person's body acting upon the knowledge of the principle, which is fueled by his or her mind having the right attitude concerning the fact.

Carla Burton

Chapter 5

Attitude

Before we begin discussing attitude, let's understand that attitude is a condition of the heart. But attitude also _ALWAYS_ shows up on the outside! Ever had to discipline your child? How about had a disagreement with your spouse? Ever forgot an important date or event? Ever said about someone, "They are so negative"? Have you ever seen someone talking and even though you couldn't hear what was being said, you could tell what kind of attitude they had? Ever had your child stomp around or slam a door? Ever had your spouse continually and deeply sigh to let you know they weren't pleased about something? If you have answered yes to any of these – then you understand that attitudes always make themselves known outwardly.

Proverbs 23:7 says, _"As a man thinketh in his heart so is he."_ That is strong language when you realize that your attitude controls your actions. Your attitude controls your emotions and your attitude controls your obedience.

The Right Attitude

Attitude determines how acceptable a person is to God and His plan. The Bible bears witness to the fact that God considers attitude to be the most important requirement for fulfilling His job descriptions. He didn't want Moses perfect, just willing; He didn't ask Abraham to understand, just to accept; He didn't want Mary to worry, just to trust; He didn't ask Peter to be tactful, just excited; and He didn't ask His flesh, Jesus, to be supportive, just to submit to the cross.

Don't confuse being flawed with having a bad attitude. Just because we have weaknesses and personal issues does not mean that we cannot have the right attitude. God's choice of people throughout the Bible shows us that He doesn't worry about flaws, but He does check out our attitude.

A perfect example is how Jesus dealt with the Pharisee's. When they came to him, they always came with a spirit of rebellion, debate, to create confusion, to try and trip Him up and to prove themselves right. They came with a judgmental, self-righteous attitude. Jesus dealt with them by not even entertaining their conversations. He called them out on their motives and their purpose. He consistently pointed out the problems with their words and actions and how the two didn't always match up. Jesus never reached to use them or called them to follow Him.

But what was different about Nicodemus, a Pharisee that we see in John chapter three? The difference was in his attitude. We know this because his attitude showed up in his actions in approaching Jesus. He approached Him humble, with an open and willing mind and heart, and a desire to really know the truth (John 3:2). Because of that Jesus dealt with him differently than the other Pharisee's. He begins to explain the plan of salvation in depth. From this conversation we get some of the most powerful scriptures for salvation that continue to illuminate our lives today. The right attitude makes all the difference in the world.

The Wrong Attitude

The Bible gives examples of men who were rejected from God's plan because they had the wrong attitude. Esau was passed over for the birthright because he didn't care about it; Saul lost the kingdom for his descendents because he didn't patiently wait for God's plan; Judas lost his life because he tried to force the hand of God; and the rich, young ruler couldn't walk with Jesus because his heart had other things first.

Holiness without a holy attitude makes a person's holiness *standards* nothing in His eyes.

When you look at the lives of these men, the difference between this list and the previous one comes down to one thing – their attitude. One list of men was flawed but had a teachable attitude. The other list was also flawed but was unwilling to learn.

The life of Cain and Able is the clearest example of this difference. They were brothers and were raised in the same home environment. They heard their parents tell the story of the garden and their sin of disobedience. They heard about how that because of this sin they had to leave the garden and work to be able to provide for their family. They heard about how that before God allowed them to leave the garden, He gave an object lesson on what they had to do to create an atmosphere where His presence could come and communicate with them. Genesis 3:21 is one of the most overlooked scriptures in the Bible. This is where God showed them by killing an animal, shedding it's blood and making a coat of skin to cover the outward symbol of the inward sinful change, that they were able to create a temporary bridge back into fellowship with Him. They obviously understood this lesson and passed it down to their sons, Cain and Able. Because we see, in

Genesis 4:3-4, that they each set up an altar and brought an offering unto God. The difference was Able followed the instruction manual and offered the right sacrifice, but Cain followed the sin of his father and mother and thought he could do it his way. God even gave him a chance to change it all before he continued down this path (Genesis 4:6-7). And how amazing that his attitude was seen outwardly because God asks him why his countenance (facial expression) had fallen. But because Cain did not have a teachable attitude, God could not use him and his life becomes cursed (Genesis 4:11-12). I want you to understand that these two young men had almost everything in common – same home, same teaching, same environment, same knowledge, and the same work ethic. But those things are not what determined their usefulness to God – it was in one's submitted, teachable attitude versus the others rebellious, unwilling-to-learn attitude. There is a saying, *"A bad attitude is like a flat tire, until you fix it you are going nowhere."* So remember attitude determine obedience and your usefulness to God.

Holiness without a holy attitude makes a person's holiness *standards* nothing in His eyes.

God's Judgment of our Attitude

God will judge our attitude, whether good or bad, useful or unusable. Jesus showed us throughout the Bible that He rewards good, teachable attitudes. In the examples of the men found with a good attitude we see that God used them in spite of their flaws but because He knew they could be taught and learn. Adam the first sinner but also the first redeemed by the shedding of blood. Moses the murderer was also the deliverer of the nation of Israel. Jacob the deceiver was also the father of Judah, the lineage of Christ. King David a man who committed a very grievous sin but God chose to anoint the son of that relationship as the next King (Bathsheba was Solomon's mother) and he was the only man called "a man after God's own heart". Samson a man who lost it all because he couldn't control his own desires was given another chance. His hair grew back, his strength returned and he was used by God to destroy more Philistines. Peter the one who emphatically denied Christ was the one chosen only 50 days later to preach the first message of salvation on the day of Pentecost (Acts 2). Paul the man who held the coat at Stephen's stoning became one of the greatest missionaries of the gospel and the writer of most of the New Testament. A good, teachable attitude will allow God to use your life.

The parable of the talents found in Matthew 25:14-30 shows us the contrast of God's judgment regarding attitude. They each received something from the master. But when he returned, only two had been useful to Him. He shows that He rewards the good and faithful servants but he condemns the slothful servant and calls him unprofitable or unusable. Just remember that your attitude will determine your judgment, so work to learn and obey.

But not only does he judge the usefulness of those with a good attitude, He also recognizes and rewards those with the wrong attitude. We see in our example of the wrong attitude, that the punishment was usually a complete separation from God's plan and presence in their lives. Cain was driven out from his family and his home. Esau lived in bitterness and anger for many years and was never given the opportunity to get the birthright back. Achan destroyed not only his own life but caused the death of his entire family. King Saul had the kingdom taken away from his lineage and wound up at the end consulting with witches to try and find the plan of God for his life. King Rehoboam took the advice of the wrong counselors and wound up losing all but a small portion of the Kingdom of Israel. Judas wound up committing suicide because he was unable to come to terms with the choices he had made. The rich, young ruler was never heard from again in scriptures. How sad to see the lives of these men fall so far. But they had the same opportunity to learn and grow from their flaws and mistakes. The problem is that they could not be taught and because of this attitude they were unable to be used by God.

The issue with us today is all in our attitude about holiness. No matter your denomination or belief system, if we never stop learning from His Word, being kind to one another and working to be obedient in our own lives, then He will consider our attitude acceptable. For some the greatest issue is whether to receive the Word and be obedient to holiness. For others it is to judge those that do not adhere to all the teaching that they feel are important. The key is that we approach all scripture with an open heart and a willing mind and an obedient spirit. If we are working to develop ourselves with this concept then we can in turn help others when they have questions.

The Apostle Paul writes the following rebuke to the Christian church in Rome: *"But why dost thou judge thy brother? or why dost thou set at nought thy brother? for we shall all stand before the judgment seat of Christ. For it is written, As I live, saith the Lord, every knee shall bow to me, and every tongue shall confess to God. So then every one of us shall give account of himself to God. Let us not therefore judge one another any more: but judge this rather, that no man put a stumblingblock or an occasion to fall in his brother's way."* (Romans 14:10-13)

We will all be judged by Christ. In John 12:48 Jesus said, *"He that rejecteth me, and receiveth not my words, hath one that judgeth him: the word that I have spoken, the same shall **judge** him in the last day."* (Emphasis added)

The Word of God must be our personal standard of judgment. We don't have time to go around and judge others when there is so much to learn from God's Word (II Corinthians 10:12). Instead we should strive to constantly make our lives more holy according to the Word of God.

Everyone will give an account of his or her own life. God will require an explanation for every word or deed that was in error. **I would hate to have to stand before God and explain why I had a bad attitude toward a brother or sister instead of a growing relationship with Him.** He will probably respond to many people's feeble explanations with, *"What business was their life to yours?"*

In fact Jesus asked Peter this same question in John 21. He and Peter had this conversation about love and feeding His sheep and then in verse 18 Jesus begins to share the end of Peter's life with him. He was telling Peter how his death was going to glorify God. And Peter, not really liking how this conversation was going, turns to Jesus and asks Him about John the Beloved. Basically Peter said to Jesus, "What about John? How will he die?" And Jesus gives us once again this concept of being accountable for ourselves and not worrying about others by telling Peter, "What is to you if I let him live until I come back again?" We must understand that our responsibility is to live our lives compared to the Word of God and under submission to the Godly authority in our lives. We have to be careful that we don't allow this judgmental society that we live in to creep into our walk as Christians. We must make sure that we are taking care of our lives and let God and the Pastor worry about everyone.

We must avoid becoming a stumblingblock in another person's life. If we look like the holiest Pentecostal and yet our attitude stinks, offending our brothers and sisters in the Lord, then we are in direct disobedience to Romans 14:13. God will hold us accountable for our attitude. The blood of any soul lost as a result of our attitude will be upon our hands! **I don't want to stand before God with blood on my hands and try to explain it away.**

I have often said this regarding holiness. I don't care where you are on the journey (you may be at mile marker 100 while others are at mile marker 1,000) but what I am interested in is WHAT DIRECTION ARE YOU WALKING?! If you are moving towards Christ then you are moving the right direction. The closer you get into His presence you WILL put off things of the world – often without having to be asked to do it. Because of this I have to understand my responsibility as a Christian to new converts or those just learning about Christ. You must get the picture of this in your mind. If they are on the road and they are moving in the direction of Christ – if I get in their face and begin to direct them on all the things they are doing wrong – where have I placed myself? I have become a stumblingblock or a roadblock or an obstacle in their continuing journey towards Christ. So many people are standing in the wrong place. They have actually placed themselves between the person and Christ. They have asked the new convert to take their eyes of Christ and look at them while they "straighten the new convert out." We have to understand that when we do this we cause that person to have to stop walking towards God, focus on us and actually go over us or around us to continue walking towards Christ.

Our responsibility is just the opposite. We are supposed to be standing behind that new convert encouraging them to continue moving in the direction they are. We need to be their best supporter and their greatest cheerleader. We need to be in their ears (not in front of their eyes) and we need to let them know they are walking the right direction, that though they may not understand everything right now just to continue seeking God, reading His Word, praying for revelation and obeying what they understand. If we are in our proper place let me show you what will happen. If that person ever decides to turn around and move in the opposite direction; NOW I become a stumblingblock to them backsliding or turning from God. We must make sure that if we are going to be a stumblingblock to someone that we are what they have to get over to backslide and not to continue in their journey towards God.

Consequences of a Wrong Attitude

In Matthew 7:1-5, Jesus says, *"**Judge** not, that ye be not judged. For with what judgment ye judge, ye shall be judged: and with what measure ye mete, it shall be measured to you again. And why beholdest thou the mote that is in thy brother's eye, but considerest not the beam that is in thine own eye? Or how wilt thou say to thy brother, Let me pull out the mote out of thine eye; and, behold, a beam is in thine own eye? Thou hypocrite, first cast* *out the beam out of thine own eye; and then shalt thou see clearly to cast out the mote out of thy brother's eye."* (Emphasis added)

Galatians 6:7 describes the principle of sowing and reaping. Principles are things that WILL HAPPEN, not might or maybe, but WILL HAPPEN. There are principles in nature such as gravity (jump out an upper window in a tall building and see if the principle doesn't stand true) and the principle of the necessity of oxygen for life (try to breathe water and live). But even more than the principles of nature, spiritual principles established in the Word of God are more certain to be true. SPIRITUAL PRINCIPLES WILL ALWAYS COME TRUE!!! Sowing what we've reaped is an infallible principle of the Word. Adam and Eve sowed rebellion and disobedience when they ate the forbidden fruit and reaped it in sin and death; Jacob sowed deceit in his dealings with Esau and his father and reaped deceit when Laban switched Leah for Rachel; and Jesus told Peter in Matthew 26:51, *"...for all they that take the sword shall perish with the sword."*

When we disobey the first half of Matthew 7:1, then we will reap the second half of Matthew 7:1. When we judge others, we can expect to be judged, not only by people on this earth but also by God in heaven. See Matthew 7:2. If we constantly judge others, then we can't get upset when we become the topic of discussion somewhere else. **Don't load the gun and then get mad because you get shot with it.**

In Matthew 7:3-5, Jesus uses an absurd scenario. Why would we allow someone who is blind try to get something out of our eye? Anyone with a beam or log in his eye is blinded by that beam, just as someone who only sees holiness his or her own way is blind to further revelation or understanding—**not compromise, but *further understanding*.** If there are still things we are learning from the Bible about everything else, then there are still things that we can learn from the Bible concerning holiness. We cannot constantly try to get our brother or sister to line up with a holiness standard when we are suffering from the bigger problem of a holiness attitude problem.

In Matthew 23:13-28, Jesus delivers a rebuke to the Pharisees. He accuses them of shutting up the kingdom of heaven for others

(v. 13) and seeking far and wide to make one convert then turning them into bitter, judgmental Pharisees just like themselves (v. 15). He calls them blind (vs. 16, 17, 19, 24, and 26) and tells them that their tithes and standards don't mean anything because they have forgotten mercy and judgment (v. 23). Then He sums it up with what relates best to the point of this lesson. He says in Matthew 23:24-28, *"Ye blind guides, which strain at a gnat, and swallow a camel.* **Woe unto you, scribes and Pharisees, hypocrites!** *for ye make clean the outside of the cup and of the platter, but within they are full of extortion and excess.* **Thou blind Pharisee,** *cleanse first that which is within the cup and platter, that the outside of them may be clean also.* **Woe unto you, scribes and Pharisees, hypocrites!** *for ye are like unto whited sepulchres,* which indeed appear beautiful outward, but are within full of dead men's bones, and of all uncleanness. Even so ye also outwardly appear righteous unto men, but within ye are full of hypocrisy and iniquity."* Each of us should substitute our names in the place of the Pharisees to see if we have a problem with an attitude of holiness.

Attitude will determine how pleasing our holiness is to God. The whole purpose of holiness it to be pleasing to God and accepted into His presence so therefore a large part of our holiness is our attitude. God was very specific in the Old Testament regarding the types and appearance of the sacrifices that were offered to Him. There were instances where someone brought a sacrifice but because they didn't offer the right one it was not accepted by Him.

In Genesis 4 we see Cain bring an offering. But God had no pleasure in Cain's offering because Cain didn't not bring the correct one. Nadab and Abihu in Leviticus 10 offered an offering of strange fire to God and they were killed. We have to understand that many people have a strict holiness standard outwardly but inside their attitude stinks. God wants us to understand that He looks at every part of us and needs to make sure that we are complete in ALL holiness standards. He wants us to understand that your outward holiness will be acceptable to Him if your inward attitude is correct. He wants you to offer Him your attitude first and then get the rest in order.

Your Perspective Affects Your Attitude

The way a person feels about holiness will be related to how that person views holiness. A person's attitude is affected by his or her perspective. The most important thing a person should remember is that God is our loving Heavenly Father and only desires the best for His children. Matthew 7:9-11 reveals how much more God loves His children than even an earthly father would love his children. If a child asks his earthly father for bread, he wouldn't be given a stone; if a child asks his father for a piece of fish, he wouldn't be given a snake. Jesus says, "If ye then, being evil, know how to give good gifts unto your children, how much more shall your Father which is in heaven give good things to them that ask him." Even more than an earthly father, Jesus wants the best for His children and He wants them to be protected from harm.

Your Prison or Your Protection

Many people view holiness as a prison. A prison is a facility built to "keep people locked or bound inside." (*Webster's Dictionary*, Landoll, 1997) It is not a place that is viewed positively, but rather it is viewed as a place to be avoided. The walls are built to keep people imprisoned or locked up so that they cannot escape and be free. If prison doors were opened, there would not be one prisoner who would remain, because it's not a place where people want to be.

When a person views holiness as a prison, then he or she will not view God as a loving father, but rather as a stern warden or taskmaster. If a person sees God as unjustly handing down sentences or standards, that person will spend all his time dreaming of escaping the prison. He will dread every moment he lives. His mind will invent ways in which he can be released.

But there are some barriers that are built for our protection. Barriers, such as fences, dams, and walls are built to protect us against predators, floods, animals, rain and other elements that might harm us. These things are put in our lives ***not to keep us in, but to keep danger out***.

When my husband and I bought our first home, our backyard was bordered by a wooded area. Our daughter, Caitlin, was about 4 years old, and she would not go out into the backyard to play or swing unless her father or I were with her. She kept telling us that she was afraid of what was in the woods. We invested in a brand new wooden fence, and from that time on, we couldn't keep her in the house. <u>The instant that she felt protected she began to feel a freedom and liberty she hadn't felt before</u>.

Holiness should be viewed as God's protection for us. God has not placed us in a prison, but He has placed a protection around us to guard us against things from the world. If we allow the world in, it will destroy us; therefore, God has given us standards of holiness as a protective barrier to keep the world out.

For instance, God instructed us to save intimacy for marriage. Today we realize how much God protected us through this standard. By living inside God's barrier regarding intimacy, we are protected from disease, sadness, and having to raise children alone instead of with two parents.

God gave us standards for what we put into our bodies. Because we choose to live inside His barrier, we are protected from being addicted to alcohol or drugs.

We must learn that God has given us holiness not to imprison us, but to liberate us. When we see holiness as a protective boundary that God established to keep us from harm, we experience liberty and freedom. John 8:32 says it best, "And ye shall know the truth, and the truth shall make you free."

Chapter 6

Principles

Unchangeable Laws

Principles are unchangeable laws that exist in the natural and the spiritual worlds. Gravity is a natural law or principle that determines the direction of moving objects within the earth's atmosphere. For example, apples fall to the ground; parachuters jump from airplanes and immediately begin to fall. The principle of gravity cannot be changed, but we have found ways to overcome the principle with great effort (e.g., airplanes and space shuttles). The plan of salvation is a basic principle or law that every person must obey to get into heaven. When a person is born again of the water and the Spirit (John 3:5), then that person has obeyed a spiritual principle; that person will receive the reward of heaven. The plan of salvation is a principle that is written in the Word of God and cannot be changed.

Subjection to Principles

Even before a person knows about the existence of a principle, he or she is subject to the power of that principle. Think about gravity. Even before Isaac Newton, sitting under the apple tree, realized the principle of gravity when the apple fell on his head, his body was subject to that principle. Isaac Newton had never floated off the ground, and if he had ever jumped off anything, his body had obeyed the law of gravity.

Even if a person doesn't know about the plan of salvation, he or she will still be subject to the principle at death. Hebrews 9:27 tells us that *"...it is appointed unto men once to die, but after this the judgment."* The verse doesn't point out any difference between those who obeyed the principle and those who did not. It says "unto men," meaning all people. So even if a person does not fully understand the principle, he or she will still be held accountable for the principle. Every person will still be under subjection to the principle's rules and rewards.

Mankind's Sinful Nature

To understand the importance of living by principle, a person must understand some basic facts concerning mankind. We are all born sinners. (Psalms 51:5, Romans 3:23) We have the nature of our father, Satan. (John 8:44) Even with the power of the Holy Ghost, it is difficult to overcome our sinful nature. (Romans 7:15-25)

First Step in Obtaining Holiness

We must first obtain salvation before we ever may obtain holiness. Every person must be born again. (John 3:3-5, Acts 2:38) A born again Christian will receive a new nature through the Holy Ghost. (II Peter 1:3, 4) With the Holy Ghost, a person has the ability to overcome sin. (Romans 6:6-7, 11-14, 17-18, 22)

Process of Holiness

Holiness means **conformity to the character of God**. It means to think as He thinks, love what He loves, hate what He hates, and act as Christ would act. (I Peter 1:15-16) Holiness is a process. (Hebrew 12:14) Moses and the children of Israel at Mt. Sinai were not all at the same level of holiness. God forbade the children of Israel to *touch* the mountain where the presence of God met with Moses. (Exodus 19:10-13) The Lord allowed Moses, Aaron, and the 70 elders to come a little further up the mountain. (Exodus 24:1, 9) Then Aaron and the elders had to stay at that point and God took Moses to the top of the mountain with Him. (Exodus 24:2, 15-18)

As Christians, we must have a certain tolerance for people who are in the process of holiness. We all are at different levels in our knowledge and understanding of God. We must trust that God and our pastor will determine those who stubbornly refuse to obey God's word.

Holiness is a continual process of sanctification (or cleansing). If a person does not continue in the process, that person will forfeit his or her born-again status. (Psalms 51:1-10)

Holiness is a two-part process: separation from this world or worldliness (II Corinthians 6:17) and dedication to God. (II Corinthians 6:18-17:1)

Separation from Worldliness

The Bible offers examples of God's call for separation of His people from the world. Abram and his family had to separate from

Ur of the Chaldees (Genesis 12:1 3); Abraham and Lot had to separate from each other (Genesis 13:8-13); and the children of Israel had to leave Egypt. (Leviticus 20:24-26)

God has always required that His people be something separate and set apart from everyone and everything else. John 15:19 says, *". . .but because you are not of the world, but I have chosen you out of the world, therefore the world hateth you."* In Romans 12:1 He tells us to that we are not to "conform" to this world but to actually be transformed (completely different) than the world around us. True holiness will show its separation from the world. This does not mean that we look at what the world is doing and then do everything different just to be separate from them. What it means is that we live our lives according to the principles of the Word of God. And we don't allow the culture, the motives and the trends of the world to guide our lives. We don't change our beliefs because the world seems to be moving in a different direction. We have to learn how to balance our lives by living in this world but not just blindly adapting our beliefs to this ever-changing culture. This is why you must build your holiness on the principles of the Word of God.

If you read the entire book of Judges it is the story of a people struggling to maintain their separation from the worldly cultures around them. When the children of Israel lived their lives and guided their actions according to the commandments of God given to Moses, then they were blessed and prospered. But then they would get their eyes off the scriptures and look at the societies around them. They would begin to act, think, look and live like them. Each time, God removed His blessings from them and they begin to decline. The children of Israel would wind up in bondage and they would cry out to God and begin to repent and cleanse themselves. Then God would send them a deliverer or someone to help them defeat their enemies. Unfortunately, the cycle would begin all over again.

We must learn the lesson of the book of Judges. God separated His people for His glory. If we are truly going to be His people and His witness, then we are going to be different from the world around us.

Dedication to God

Separation from the world is essential for obtaining holiness, but it is not enough. God expects us to dedicate all of ourselves unto Him. Romans 12:1-2 tells us to present our bodies as a "living sacrifice." Remember that a living sacrifice can get off the altar, and that is why holiness is a continual dedication to God each day. Ephesians 4:22-24 encourages us to put off the things of the old man, and being renewed, take on the new man created in righteousness. God desires us to dedicate our lives continually unto Him.

It is not enough that we just separate from the world, that is only one-half of the equation. The problem with a lot of people in regarding holiness, is that work on only the separation part of the problem. They strive to be as different from the world as possible. But they do this more as an obligation unto God. His desire is that we not only be willing and have understanding regarding our need to be separate from the world, but that we also strive to dedicate our lives to Him.

Dedication to God is learning to love Him with all your heart. It is studying to show yourself approved by learning and understanding the principle and purpose behind holiness standards. Holiness was not designed to be lived only from a "separation" standpoint. God wants us to desire to do holiness because we have an understanding of the principle from the Word of God and a love in our hearts to be more like Him. This is what dedication unto God means.

The Lesson Of The Children Of Israel

To understand this concept of separation from the world and dedication to God, we have to look no further than the Children of Israel. God had sent them a Deliverer to lead them out (separation) from Egypt. Even though there was a temporary struggle for them to accomplish this – they did succeed. They came out of Egypt and even saw several victories along the way.

However, they found the dedication to God process so much more difficult. As they pursued separation there came a point where God desired more than just that – He desired them to dedicate (trust, follow). He wanted them to complete the mission He started in their lives. They were never intended to just run away from the world. And so they found themselves standing on the door of Canaan. This was the place where they could rest and develop a permanent, close relationship with God. But whereas coming out of Egypt was only slightly difficult, they found the dedication part of this process insurmountable. In fact the first time they found themselves here, they didn't succeed in completing the dedication part of this process. It would take 40 more years of running and separating from the world before they were ready to attempt dedication again.

We have to understand how important BOTH parts of this process are to God. Because without the separation from the world *AND* the dedication to God we have not completed true holiness.

Holiness means having no love in your heart for this world. God says that we are committing adultery against Him when we love the world more than Him. (James 4:4)

Holiness involves two parts of us: Inward Holiness—Spirit and Soul and Outward Holiness—Body. (I Corinthians 6:19-20; I Thessalonians 5:23; II Corinthians 7:1)

The Issue or the Principle

The reason that many Christians have trouble obeying the holiness standards long term is because they are focused on the issue and not the principle. They are consumed by how the issue is affecting them, versus being able to understand the need to obey the principle behind the issue. Each time that God demanded a holiness separation from His people, there was a spiritual principle behind it. **<u>My greatest fear is that we are raising a generation that is trying to obey the issue without grasping the principle.</u>** The principle is the foundation that will ground you when people question your actions, or when you have doubts, fears and frustrations.

The issue is the action or the outward standard that we obey. *But the issue is not the principle.* The scripture is clear on the subject of men and women's hair. Cutting or not cutting the hair is the issue but it is not the principle. The principle is submission to authority and what we do with our hair is just the evidence that we are in direct obedience or disobedience to the principle. I will share more regarding this specific principle later on in this book.

The issue is speaking with other tongues but that is not the principle. The principle is salvation and tongues is simply the outward evidence (standard) that we have obeyed the Biblical principle.

Don't get so consumed with the issues that you miss the principle. The principle is the foundation that we build our lives upon. The issue is simply the outward evidence that we have understood and obeyed the principle from the Word of God.

Carla Burton

Chapter 7

Standards

Christians develop personal standards for living when they dedicate their lives to God. Standards separate Christians from the world. Standards fall under two categories: inward holiness and outward holiness.

Inward Holiness

Standards for inward holiness include the way a person thinks and speaks and personal beliefs about where he or she may not go or things in which he or she may not participate, such as drugs, alcohol, pornography, gambling, etc. It also involves smaller inward acts of holiness such as guarding our tongues, keeping a right spirit, renewing our minds, and keeping unity among the brethren. Often, inward holiness is harder to maintain than outward holiness because there are things ingrained in our actions and character. This is where we must be completely "transformed" as Paul commands us in Romans 12:2.

Some standards are explicitly stated in the Word of God; some standards develop as a result of cultural circumstances. For instance, when television was first made available to the public, the programming was not ungodly. Now television is a vehicle for sinful man to parade extremely ungodly messages and visual content in front of the viewer. It is indiscriminate in whom it affects; nudity and perversion are now a common theme for prime time television, a time that families usually spend together in front of the tube. As a result, most pastors now condemn the use of TV for entertainment.

Standards may differ slightly for each Christian at any given time because holiness is a process. However, a pastor may feel led of God to dictate certain standards for the general benefit of his congregation.

Outward Holiness

Outward, or physical, standards pertain to a dress code and should reflect an inward holiness standard of modesty.*

Because holiness is a process and because Jesus tells us

---

* Specific inward and outward holiness standards are addressed in booklets written by Carla Burton dedicated to those subjects.

that it begins inwardly, more often than not, outward standards can take a while to manifest themselves in new converts. Just remember that this is process (remember Mt. Sinai) and you have to give time, teaching and the process of illumination for the new convert. However, outward holiness is also a sign of the condition of someone who has been walking with God for a while.

In using the example of the Shepherd, we see that the only way he knows that something is wrong with the sheep in his care is by their outward actions. If there is a sheep that is active, in the front of the fold, playing, eating well, and whose coat looks healthy, then the Shepherd knows that most likely that sheep is okay. However, if that same sheep all of the sudden is lethargic, not excited, straggling along behind the fold and with outward signs that they are sick, the Shepherd becomes concerned that something is wrong inwardly. So God does use our outward holiness standards (giving, dress, hair, worship, ministry, attendance) to let the Pastor know when someone is moving in the wrong direction. Remember the example I gave you previously about being a stumblingblock for someone moving in the wrong direction. That is the Pastor's job in your life; to be your spiritual thermometer and let you know when you are moving in the wrong direction. Outward holiness is often the first signs that God gives a Pastor to know your spiritual condition.

The cause of Lucifer's fall began inwardly but then manifested itself outwardly (Ezekiel 28). Cain's outward countenance reflected his inward thought process (Genesis

4). We can never discount inward or outward holiness but realize that they work together as the evidence of our understanding of the principle behind the issue.

Carla Burton

Chapter 8

Living *in Holiness*

Now that we've seen that the order of holiness is vitally important to God, let's see how we should live. In Luke 6:36-45, Jesus tells us how we should live if we want to produce a holiness that will make us acceptable to Him and to His plan for our lives. He says, *"Be ye therefore **merciful**, as your Father also is **merciful**. **Judge not, and ye shall not be judged: condemn not, and ye shall not be condemned: forgive, and ye shall be forgiven:** For a good tree bringeth not forth corrupt fruit; neither doth a corrupt tree bring forth good fruit. For every tree is known by his own fruit. For of thorns men do not gather figs, nor of a bramble bush gather they grapes. A good man out of the good treasure of his heart bringeth forth that which is good; and an evil man out of the evil treasure of his heart bringeth forth that which is evil: **for of the abundance of the heart his mouth speaketh**"*

Be Merciful!

If we are merciful, then God can also be merciful to us when we fail—not *if* we fail, but *when* we fail. We cannot be perfect. We will all be in need of mercy one day, so be sure to show mercy every day! In Matthew 5:7, Jesus tells us that merciful people are blessed because they can obtain mercy.

Don't Judge Others!

In Luke 6, Jesus tells us not to judge so that we won't be judged; not to condemn so that we won't be condemned; and to forgive so that we can be forgiven. We cannot receive blessings and goodness and longsuffering and understanding unless we are willing to give blessings and goodness and longsuffering and understanding. It is the principle of sowing and reaping again.

Plant the Right Seeds!

Just as we can sow and reap bad things, we can also sow and reap good things. But remember that whatever we sow WE WILL REAP AGAIN. In Luke 6:38-45, Jesus explains that trees produce what is in the seed. If we want God and others to be longsuffering with us, then we must return the favor. If we have seeds of judgment and condemnation in our hearts, then those things are definitely being produced by our mouths and lives. Remember that every time we speak, we are sowing seeds in the lives of the people around us. Whatever spirit or attitude we produce our children will also produce. People who say that everyone is always talking about them or their children should check their mouths and homes; they are probably reaping what they have sown. Jesus ended these words, ". . . *for of the abundance of the heart his mouth speaketh."* Look out mouth, you're telling on me!

Hebrews 12:14

Follow peace with all men, **and holiness**, without which no man shall see the Lord:

I Peter 1:15-16

But as he which hath called you is **holy**, so be ye **holy** in all manner of conversation; Because it is written, Be ye **holy**; for I am **holy**.

2 Corinthians 6:17

Wherefore come out from among them, **and be ye separate**, saith the Lord, and touch not the unclean thing; and I will receive you.

2 Corinthians 7:1

Having therefore these promises, dearly beloved, let us cleanse ourselves from all filthiness of the flesh and spirit, **perfecting holiness in the fear of God.**

Made in the USA
Middletown, DE
15 June 2021